my Favorite Plays

A journal for theatre lovers

Tara Kachaturoff

Dedication

This book is dedicated to those who love to experience life in all its nuances. Enjoy!

"The stage is not merely the meeting place of all the arts, but is also the return of art to life."
~ Oscar Wilde

My Theatre Thoughts

Play Rating

Play ____________________

Date ____________________

Venue ____________________

Attended with ____________________

Summary ____________________

more thoughts ...

My Theatre Thoughts

Play Rating

Play ______________________________

Date ______________________________

Venue ______________________________

Attended with ______________________________

____

Summary ______________________________

more thoughts ...

My Theatre Thoughts

Play Rating

Play ______________________________

Date ______________________________

Venue ______________________________

Attended with ______________________________

Summary ______________________________

more thoughts ...

My Theatre Thoughts

Play Rating

Play ______________________________________

Date ______________________________________

Venue _____________________________________

Attended with ______________________________

____

Summary ___________________________________

more thoughts ...

My Theatre Thoughts

Play Rating

Play ______________________________

Date ______________________________

Venue ______________________________

Attended with ______________________________

Summary ______________________________

more thoughts ...

My Theatre Thoughts

Play Rating

Play ____________________________________

Date ____________________________________

Venue ____________________________________

Attended with ______________________________

____

Summary ____________________________________

more thoughts ...

My Theatre Thoughts

Play Rating

Play ______________________________

Date ______________________________

Venue ______________________________

Attended with ______________________________

____

Summary ______________________________

more thoughts ...

My Theatre Thoughts

Play Rating

Play ____________________

Date ____________________

Venue ____________________

Attended with ____________________

____

Summary ____________________

more thoughts ...

My Theatre Thoughts

Play Rating

Play ______________________________________

Date ______________________________________

Venue ______________________________________

Attended with ______________________________

____

Summary ____________________________________

more thoughts ...

My Theatre Thoughts

Play Rating

Play ____

Date ____

Venue ____

Attended with ____

____

Summary ____

more thoughts ...

My Theatre Thoughts

Play Rating

Play ____

Date ____

Venue ____

Attended with ____

____

Summary ____

more thoughts ...

My Theatre Thoughts

Play Rating

Play ______________________________

Date ______________________________

Venue ______________________________

Attended with ______________________________

Summary ______________________________

more thoughts ...

My Theatre Thoughts

Play Rating

Play ____

Date ____

Venue ____

Attended with ____________________________________

Summary ____

more thoughts ...

My Theatre Thoughts

Play Rating

Play

Date

Venue

Attended with

Summary

more thoughts ...

My Theatre Thoughts

Play Rating

Play

Date

Venue

Attended with

Summary

more thoughts ...

My Theatre Thoughts

Play Rating

Play ______________________________

Date ______________________________

Venue ______________________________

Attended with ______________________________

Summary ______________________________

more thoughts ...

My Theatre Thoughts

Play Rating

Play ________________________________

Date ________________________________

Venue ________________________________

Attended with ________________________________

Summary ________________________________

more thoughts ...

My Theatre Thoughts

Play Rating

Play ______________________________

Date ______________________________

Venue ______________________________

Attended with ______________________________

Summary ______________________________

more thoughts ...

My Theatre Thoughts

Play Rating

Play ______________________________________

Date ______________________________________

Venue ______________________________________

Attended with ______________________________

____

Summary ______________________________________

____

____

____

____

____

____

____

____

____

____

____

____

____

____

____

____

____

____

____

more thoughts ...

My Theatre Thoughts

Play Rating

Play ______________________________________

Date ______________________________________

Venue ______________________________________

Attended with ______________________________

____

Summary ___________________________________

____

____

____

____

____

____

____

____

____

____

____

____

____

____

____

____

____

____

____

more thoughts ...

My Theatre Thoughts

Play Rating

Play ______________________________

Date ______________________________

Venue ______________________________

Attended with ______________________________

____

Summary ______________________________

more thoughts ...

My Theatre Thoughts

Play Rating

Play ______________________________

Date ______________________________

Venue ______________________________

Attended with ______________________________

Summary ______________________________

more thoughts ...

My Theatre Thoughts

Play Rating

Play ____

Date ____

Venue ____

Attended with ____________________________________

____

Summary _______________________________________

more thoughts ...

My Theatre Thoughts

Play Rating

Play ______________________________

Date ______________________________

Venue ______________________________

Attended with ______________________________

____

Summary ______________________________

more thoughts ...

My Theatre Thoughts

Play Rating

Play ______________________________

Date ______________________________

Venue ______________________________

Attended with ______________________________

____

Summary ______________________________

more thoughts ...

My Theatre Thoughts

Play Rating

Play ____

Date ____

Venue ____

Attended with ____________________________________

____

Summary ____

more thoughts ...

My Theatre Thoughts

Play Rating

Play ____

Date ____

Venue ____

Attended with ______________________________________

____

Summary ____

____

____

____

____

____

____

____

____

____

____

____

____

____

____

____

____

____

____

____

more thoughts ...

My Theatre Thoughts

Play Rating

Play ________________________________

Date ________________________________

Venue ________________________________

Attended with ________________________________

____

Summary ________________________________

more thoughts ...

My Theatre Thoughts

Play Rating

Play

Date

Venue

Attended with

Summary

more thoughts ...

My Theatre Thoughts

Play Rating

Play ____

Date ____

Venue ____

Attended with ______________________________________

____

Summary ____

____

____

____

____

____

____

____

____

____

____

____

____

____

____

____

____

____

____

____

more thoughts ...

My Theatre Thoughts

Play Rating

Play ______________________________________

Date ______________________________________

Venue ______________________________________

Attended with ______________________________________

____

Summary ______________________________________

more thoughts ...

My Theatre Thoughts

Play Rating

Play ____

Date ____

Venue ____

Attended with _____________________________________

Summary ____

more thoughts ...

My Theatre Thoughts

Play Rating

Play ______________________________

Date ______________________________

Venue ______________________________

Attended with ______________________________

Summary ______________________________

more thoughts ...

My Theatre Thoughts

Play Rating

Play

Date

Venue

Attended with

Summary

more thoughts ...

My Theatre Thoughts

Play Rating

Play ______________________________

Date ______________________________

Venue ______________________________

Attended with ______________________________

____

Summary ______________________________

more thoughts ...

My Theatre Thoughts

Play Rating

Play

Date

Venue

Attended with

Summary

more thoughts ...

My Theatre Thoughts

Play Rating

Play ______________________________

Date ______________________________

Venue ______________________________

Attended with ______________________________

____

Summary ______________________________

more thoughts ...

My Theatre Thoughts

Play Rating

Play ______________________________

Date ______________________________

Venue ______________________________

Attended with ______________________________

____

Summary ______________________________

more thoughts ...

My Theatre Thoughts

Play Rating

Play ______________________________

Date ______________________________

Venue ______________________________

Attended with ______________________________

Summary ______________________________

more thoughts ...

My Theatre Thoughts

Play Rating

Play ____

Date ____

Venue ____

Attended with ____________________________________

Summary ____

more thoughts ...

My Theatre Thoughts

Play Rating

Play ____________________

Date ____________________

Venue ____________________

Attended with ____________________

Summary ____________________

more thoughts ...

My Theatre Thoughts

Play Rating

Play ____

Date ____

Venue _______________________________________

Attended with __________________________________

Summary ____________________________________

more thoughts ...

My Theatre Thoughts

Play Rating

Play ____

Date ____

Venue ____

Attended with ____________________________________

Summary ______________________________________

more thoughts ...

My Theatre Thoughts

Play Rating

Play ______________________________

Date ______________________________

Venue ______________________________

Attended with ______________________________

Summary ______________________________

more thoughts ...

My Theatre Thoughts

Play Rating

Play ______________________________________

Date ______________________________________

Venue ______________________________________

Attended with ______________________________

Summary ___________________________________

more thoughts ...

My Theatre Thoughts

Play Rating

Play ____________________________________

Date ____________________________________

Venue ____________________________________

Attended with ____________________________

____

Summary ____________________________________

more thoughts ...

My Theatre Thoughts

Play Rating

Play ______________________________

Date ______________________________

Venue ______________________________

Attended with ______________________________

____

Summary ______________________________

more thoughts ...

My Theatre Thoughts

Play Rating

Play ______________________________________

Date ______________________________________

Venue ______________________________________

Attended with ______________________________

____

Summary ___________________________________

more thoughts ...

My Theatre Thoughts

Play Rating

Play ____

Date ____

Venue ____

Attended with ____

____

Summary ____

more thoughts ...

My Theatre Thoughts

Play Rating

Play ______________________________

Date ______________________________

Venue ______________________________

Attended with ______________________________

____

Summary ______________________________

more thoughts ...

My Theatre Thoughts

Play Rating

Play ______________________________

Date ______________________________

Venue ______________________________

Attended with ______________________________

____

Summary ______________________________

more thoughts ...

My Theatre Thoughts

Play Rating

Play ____________________

Date ____________________

Venue ____________________

Attended with ____________________

Summary ____________________

more thoughts ...

My Theatre Thoughts

Play Rating

Play ______________________________

Date ______________________________

Venue ______________________________

Attended with ______________________________

Summary ______________________________

more thoughts ...

My Theatre Thoughts

Play Rating

Play ____

Date ____

Venue ____

Attended with ____________________________________

Summary ______________________________________

more thoughts ...

My Theatre Thoughts

Play Rating

Play ____

Date ____

Venue ____

Attended with ________________________________

____

Summary ______________________________________

more thoughts ...

My Theatre Thoughts

Play Rating

Play ____

Date ____

Venue ____

Attended with ____

____

Summary ____

____

____

____

____

____

____

____

____

____

____

____

____

____

____

____

____

____

____

more thoughts ...

My Theatre Thoughts

Play Rating

Play ______________________________

Date ______________________________

Venue ______________________________

Attended with ______________________________

____

Summary ______________________________

more thoughts ...

My Theatre Thoughts

Play Rating

Play ______________________________

Date ______________________________

Venue ______________________________

Attended with ______________________________

____

Summary ______________________________

more thoughts ...

My Theatre Thoughts

Play Rating

Play

Date

Venue

Attended with

Summary

more thoughts ...

My Theatre Thoughts

Play Rating

Play ______________________________

Date ______________________________

Venue ______________________________

Attended with ______________________________

____

Summary ______________________________

more thoughts ...

My Theatre Thoughts

Play Rating

Play ______________________________

Date ______________________________

Venue ______________________________

Attended with ______________________________

____

Summary ______________________________

more thoughts ...

My Theatre Thoughts

Play Rating

Play ______________________________

Date ______________________________

Venue ______________________________

Attended with ______________________________

____

Summary ______________________________

more thoughts ...

My Theatre Thoughts

Play Rating

Play ______________________________

Date ______________________________

Venue ______________________________

Attended with ______________________________

____

Summary ______________________________

more thoughts ...

My Theatre Thoughts

Play Rating

Play ____________________

Date ____________________

Venue ____________________

Attended with ____________________

____

Summary ____________________

more thoughts ...

My Theatre Thoughts

Play Rating

Play ______________________________

Date ______________________________

Venue ______________________________

Attended with ______________________________

____

Summary ______________________________

more thoughts ...

My Theatre Thoughts

Play Rating

Play ______________________________

Date ______________________________

Venue ______________________________

Attended with ______________________________

Summary ______________________________

more thoughts ...

My Theatre Thoughts

Play Rating

Play ____

Date ____

Venue ____

Attended with ____

____

Summary ____

more thoughts ...

My Theatre Thoughts

Play Rating

Play

Date

Venue

Attended with

Summary

more thoughts ...

My Theatre Thoughts

Play Rating

Play ______________________________

Date ______________________________

Venue ______________________________

Attended with ______________________________

____

Summary ______________________________

more thoughts ...

My Theatre Thoughts

Play Rating

Play ____

Date ____

Venue ____

Attended with ______________________________________

____

Summary ____

____

____

____

____

____

____

____

____

____

____

____

____

____

____

____

____

____

____

____

____

more thoughts ...

My Theatre Thoughts

Play Rating

Play ______________________________________

Date ______________________________________

Venue ______________________________________

Attended with ______________________________________

____

Summary ______________________________________

more thoughts ...

My Theatre Thoughts

Play Rating

Play

Date

Venue

Attended with

Summary

more thoughts ...

My Theatre Thoughts

Play Rating

Play ______________________________

Date ______________________________

Venue ______________________________

Attended with ______________________________

Summary ______________________________

more thoughts ...

My Theatre Thoughts

Play Rating

Play ______________________________

Date ______________________________

Venue ______________________________

Attended with ______________________________

____

Summary ______________________________

more thoughts ...

My Theatre Thoughts

Play Rating

Play ______________________________

Date ______________________________

Venue ______________________________

Attended with ______________________________

____

Summary ______________________________

more thoughts ...

My Theatre Thoughts

Play Rating

Play ____

Date ____

Venue ____

Attended with ____________________________________

Summary ______________________________________

more thoughts ...

28850362R00088

Made in the USA
Columbia, SC
17 October 2018